Church Floors
and
Floor Coverings

by
Daryl Fowler

D1547265

Published for the Council for the Care of Churches by

CHURCH HOUSE PUBLISHING
Church House, Great Smith Street, London SW1P 3NZ

ISBN 0 7151 7563 7

Published 1992 for the Council for the Care of Churches
by Church House Publishing

Printed in England by Tasprint Ltd.

CONTENTS

INTRODUCTION

The floor of a church tends to be taken for granted but, like the roof, it is there to serve an essential function. Primarily it forms a level firm platform on which we can walk and kneel in comfort. Many of our church floors also contain important monuments, brasses and tiles, both plain and decorated, that are a vital part of our heritage and contribute much to the interest and beauty of our churches. Yet all too often they are damaged by a combination of neglect, ignorance and, sadly, theft.

The aim of this booklet is to help those who care for our parish churches and who have to look after both historic and modern floor finishes, and to assist in the selection of new finishes when they are necessary.

The author and the Council for the Care of Churches are grateful to Mr Kenneth Beaulah, Shire Publications Ltd, the Trustees of the British Museum and the Musée de Saint-Omer for granting permission for drawings to be used. The author is also indebted to Miss Hazel Newey for commenting on the section on metal floor coverings.

ARCHAEOLOGICAL AND ART-HISTORICAL ASPECTS

Properly understood, the church floor is an area which will assist in the unravelling of the historical development of the church building through the centuries. Any proposals to alter or disturb areas of flooring that have been untouched for many years must involve the Diocesan Archaeological Consultant, who will be able to interpret the evidence contained there.

Early church floors bore little resemblance to those of today. For an ordinary parish church earth was the ubiquitous material, renewed again and again. This is revealed to the archaeologist as a thin series of layers, often of differing colours. Occasionally there may be a major new floor either of tiles or perhaps of rammed chalk or of clay and blood mixed together. These floors were seldom level. Indeed, our concept of level floors with steps is a relatively new idea. Slopes both across and along the length of the church of up to half a metre in depth appear to have been not uncommon.

Modern excavation techniques can recover the position of features or the arrangement of fittings – for example, where the benches, the font or the doors were situated in the thirteenth or fourteenth centuries. In many villages the parish church was the largest roofed building, and it is not unusual to find that industrial processes have taken place in the nave. If a new bell was to be cast, the casting pit would have been dug in the middle of the floor and a small furnace would have been provided.

The floor levels would originally have related to the architectural features, but as generations passed, earth floors would rise, sometimes to a height of several feet. The restorers of our churches generally levelled these out and it is now quite rare to find a surviving earth floor, except when they are hidden under nineteenth-century wooden pew platforms.

Floors commonly found in parish churches today are composed of paving laid with stone, marble or brick paviors, or pavement tiles. Wood floors are frequently found under pews, or where pews have been removed. Some monuments are commonly found set into church floors – stone ledger slabs commemorating burials are an important part of the record of the burial and often correspond to vaults located beneath. Slabs may have incorporated monumental brasses which sometimes survive. More often, the brass will be gone and the stone slab will have only an indent where the brass was located.

The other group of monuments commonly found on church floors is mediaeval coffin slabs. Solid stone coffins were quite common in some areas during the Middle Ages and, although nineteenth-century restorations often disturbed these burials, the lid of the coffin was frequently set back into the floor. Both ledger slabs and coffin slabs are thick and heavy, and any suggestion of disturbing them should be treated with caution. In any event, advice should be sought from the Diocesan Advisory Committee.

TILES

Mediaeval floor tiles fall into six main classes.

1. The earliest are plain tiles of varying shapes cut around a metal template and laid to form mosaic patterns. The first large group surviving in England, at Fountains Abbey, dates from the first quarter of the thirteenth century.

2. An elaboration of this method is found in decorated tile mosaics which form complicated pictorial scenes, such as those in Prior Crauden's Chapel of 1324 at Ely Cathedral.

3. Pseudo-mosaic tiles have incised lines to suggest the smaller tesserae, and are decorated with a white slip.

4. Tiles with relief and counter-relief decoration are rare in England, and are principally found in the eastern parts of the country and date from the thirteenth and fourteenth centuries.

Tile from Prior Crauden's Chapel, Ely Cathedral

5. Tiles with linear decoration impressed by wooden dies and filled with white slip date from the fourteenth to the sixteenth centuries.

6. The most popular type, however, beginning in the fourteenth century is the two-coloured tile in which the pattern is formed almost without exception by white clay set into the red ground.

We know from excavations that tiles were used not only in pavements, but also in small areas, for example to cover or outline an important grave or to surround a specific object such as the font.

Mediaeval tiles, formed by a wooden stamp, then infilled with a white clay slip

3

The dissolution of the monasteries in 1550 deprived the mediaeval tile industry of its main customers and, along with a change in fashion, contributed to its demise. By 1550 polychrome faience and tin-glaze tiles were being imported from the Low Countries and from Spain, but these were not designed for foot traffic and were unsuitable for pavements. In North Devon a local tile industry producing embossed and slip decorated tiles carried on into the early eighteenth century.

Tiles from North Devon of the seventeenth and eighteenth centuries, decorated in relief

Minton tile from the Temple Church, London

By the nineteenth century, antiquarian study of the past caused a renewal of interest in tiles, and this coincided with Samuel Wright's discovery of the manufacturing method of inlaid tiles. The interest of the major architects in the 1840s and '50s, for example at Jesus College, Cambridge, Cheadle Church, Staffordshire, and the Temple Church, London, led rapidly to major growth in the tile-making industry which continues today.

Nineteenth-century tiles soon achieved a considerable stylistic variety with a wide range of patterns and colours although, being mass-produced, they never achieved the same appearance of subtle variety as a mediaeval pavement. Nineteenth- and early twentieth-century floor and wall tiling now merit careful conservation.

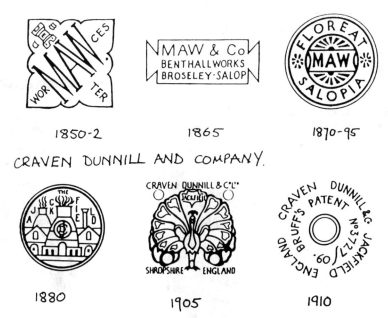

MAW AND COMPANY

1850-2   1865   1870-95

CRAVEN DUNNILL AND COMPANY.

1880   1905   1910

Victorian tile manufacturers' stamps

The materials of nineteenth-century tiles were different from those used for earlier tiles. The clays came from more than one source and were blended by machine after the arrival of mechanisation in the tile industry in the 1820s and 1830s. The screwed presses also produced a much denser consistency, and the technique for laying the tiles was different because they were often laid in Portland cement and patent mortars which are harder than their mediaeval counterparts. This makes the tiles more difficult, though not impossible, to lift. The designs are intricate, and minor variations give clues to different makers. Identification is also helped by stamps which are often present on the backs of the tiles.

It is important to remember that mediaeval tile floors survive in England to an extent unparalleled elsewhere in Europe. In France, where the mediaeval tile industry was as large as that of this country,

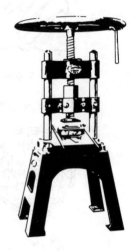

Tile Press

The Blunger. For mixing types of clay

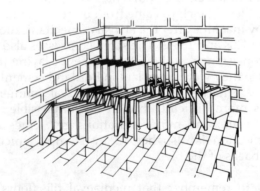

Stacking of tiles in the kiln. The kiss marks are
frequently visible on the edges of tiles

Major centres of tile manufacture in the mediaeval period

7

only seven tile pavements survive *in situ*. Worcester Cathedral alone has seven pavements, and there are dozens of others all over the country. Amongst French parish churches, so far as it is known, there is only one surviving tile pavement (and even that has been relaid), but there are hundreds in the United Kingdom. The problems of protection and conservation of mediaeval tiled floors therefore must be considered very seriously. They have recently begun to attract more than academic interest, and theft is becoming a problem.

Possibly the principal reason for the high rate of survival is that there was little change in our parish churches between the Reformation and the nineteenth century. Therefore, although the tiles were often stolen or simply thrown away, many have survived up to today.

Major pavements in their original positions present particular maintenance problems. Some of the fine examples in our cathedrals and abbeys have not been walked upon for many generations. In other areas there are replica pavements, for example in the Chapter House

Subtleties in nineteenth-century design changes

at Salisbury. Unfortunately enthusiastic attention over the years can cause significant problems. For example, a layer of wax can build up until it is several millimetres thick and can only be removed by an expensive programme of cleaning and conservation to reveal again the pavement's true glory. The laying of electricity cables can significantly damage a perfect mediaeval pavement; in such cases making good must be done with the tiles that have been removed, otherwise the pattern and, more importantly, the historical evidence will be falsified. Areas of tiling must not be muddled up. It must also be remembered that tiles themselves vary widely in thickness,

consistency and fragility. Inlaid or, more properly, encaustic, tiles can have as much as 4mm inlay of white on red tiles, as at Gloucester, and can be very thin. Some eroded pavements at Winchester show that 5mm of wear has occurred in the last seven centuries, and tiles discovered in perfect condition as recently as the 1930s which were relaid in the line of pedestrian traffic have now almost entirely lost their pattern through wear. Even replica tiles

Pseudo mosaic tiles

which were laid by Professor Baker in 1975 now show significant wear, and in many places their glaze has been totally removed.

It might be thought that an easy solution to a problem floor would be to send the tiles to a museum. Unfortunately that divorces them from their context and diminishes the value of their surroundings.

Relaid tiles can be damaged in a variety of ways – by damp or sulphates rising from below, by erosion from walking feet and by having heavy furniture dragged over them. If they are suffering, intervention will be needed to protect the pavement for the future.

Scraffito decoration on a fourteenth-century tile from Tring, Hertfordshire

9

In some cases tiles are salvaged and set in panels to hang on the wall. Many of these have inadequate rebates which may allow tiles to fall out and become loose objects in the church. Many eighteenth-century floors frequently have poorly fired clay tiles where large inclusions in the body of the tiles can work loose and come out, but despite the comparatively poor quality of the tiles, a surprising number of these floors have survived.

Reconstruction of the plain tile mosaic from Meaux Abbey, mid-thirteenth century

Tiles have a financial, as well as an art-historical, value. Although the earliest recorded sales of mediaeval tiles were from Bordesley Abbey, Redditch, in September 1559, it was not until the 1850s that great collections began to be formed. The prices of tiles today vary dramatically, but all have shown a significant growth. Tiles are undoubtedly at risk and must be recorded before they are either worn out or stolen.

Recording

Recording tiles is not as simple as it may sound. Tiles are particularly awkward objects to draw. Experience shows that the drawings available in museums are difficult to use because of problems of interpretation. It is therefore essential that photographs are used, where possible supplemented by rubbings, for example using graphite and cigarette paper. For record purposes the back of the tile is often as important as the front, and the edges can give clues to the manufacturing process and therefore to the date. (The recording of tiles is co-ordinated by the National Tile Census organised by Dr Christopher Norton at the University of York's Centre for Mediaeval Studies, The King's Manor, York, YO1 2EP.)

If the pavements have to be lifted they must be handled professionally, not by a general builder. In order to record the position of individual tiles before lifting, a tracing rather like a brass rubbing will need to be made. Scale drawings stylishly done tend to prove

10

totally useless, and full-size rubbings of the entire pavement may have to be made on which each tile must be individually located and numbered. Before being lifted and put into a pallet, each tile should be traced, and an individual rubbing should be made of it in addition to the overall rubbing showing the tile locations. The top decoration of the surface can be protected by paper tissues built up in several layers using fungicidal Polycell as the adhesive.

THE CARE AND REPAIR OF EXISTING FLOORS

Substructure

Floors may be divided into two types, according to the method of support: solid floors and suspended floors.

Solid floors

The flooring material is laid on a solid base which is intended to rest on the earth and which must remain evenly supported. Such floors are made of earth, rammed chalk, lime concrete or modern Portland cement concrete.

The frequent burials likely to have taken place under old floors will have resulted in a ground surface that has uneven bearing capabilities. Solid floor slabs may fracture over the hard areas and sink into soft areas. Modern slabs tend to be rigid and they will fracture if they are incapable of spanning the areas concerned, but a mediaeval floor will tend to settle and become uneven, giving a texture to the floor which will often appear picturesque, but may well also require patch repairs. Because they are laid directly on the ground, solid floors are susceptible to damp. Although the severity of this will vary from church to church, the control of damp, especially in mediaeval churches, is usually a question of balance. In extreme cases there may be no alternative but to replace the floor. In many buildings the factors which must be considered are the amount of damp that can be tolerated, the effect of it on the fabric and the cost of any intervention.

Modern Portland cement concrete slabs will incorporate a damp proof membrane either within or underneath the slab. Thin membranes are occasionally laid incorrectly or become punctured by subsequent building work. They do not, however, prevent the damp from penetrating other areas of the building. Modern buildings are designed so that the damp proofing is effective right across the building from external wall to external wall. New floors in old buildings seldom achieve this. It has frequently been noticed that in churches where concrete slabs have been laid the problem of rising damp in the wall can increase. Because the balance of evaporation and moisture movement is altered by the new floor slab, extra moisture becomes concentrated elsewhere in the building.

Modern floor slabs can be designed to span both hard and soft areas, but occasionally this fails and the slab will crack. There are several methods of injecting an adhesive grout into the resulting cracks, but they are unlikely to reinstate the original strength. To achieve that may involve major renewals, on which the advice of the inspecting architect should be sought.

Suspended floors

Many church floors have timber joists resting on low brick sleeper walls at ground floor level or on structural systems of several types in first floor galleries. The key to proper care of any timber floor structure at ground level is ventilation. Pew platforms without arrangements for ventilation will eventually rot from fungal attack, some more quickly than others, depending upon the moisture content of the ground beneath and the efficiency or otherwise of the rainwater disposal system. Wood rot and wood boring beetle attacks cause considerable damage to all timber structures, and vigilance is essential.

Timber platforms, at ground and first floor level, with excessive bounce should be checked. If the problem is not decay, it may be the result of a plumber or electrician cutting away too much timber from the joists to pass pipes or cables through them. Occasionally at first floor level the joists may simply not be adequate. By today's standards some timbers were undersized, and notching makes matters worse. Unfortunately, it is very difficult to make reliable structural calculations in many historic structures. It is essential to seek the advice of an architect skilled in the repair of such buildings to avoid unnecessary work.

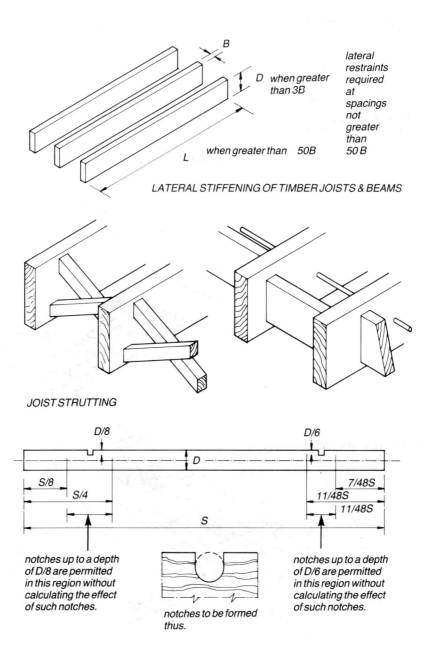

B

D when greater
than 3B

lateral
restraints
required
at
spacings
not
greater
than
50 B

when greater than   50B

L

LATERAL STIFFENING OF TIMBER JOISTS & BEAMS

JOIST STRUTTING

D/8

D/6

D

S/8

S/4

7/48S

11/48S

11/48S

S

notches up to a depth
of D/8 are permitted
in this region without
calculating the effect
of such notches.

notches to be formed
thus.

notches up to a depth
of D/6 are permitted
in this region without
calculating the effect
of such notches.

13

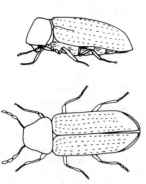

Common furniture beetle

Ensuring ventilation to floor voids is essential

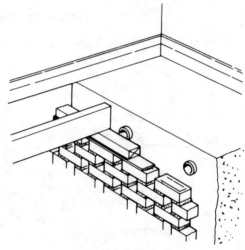

Ventilation to under-floor spaces

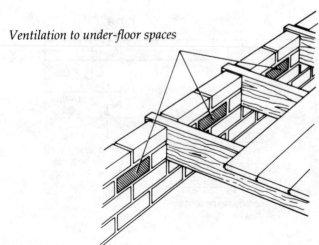

Housekeeping

Part of the secret of looking after any floor is quite simply to keep it clean. But inappropriate cleaning often does more harm than good. People bring in a large amount of abrasive dust on their shoes and spread it all over the floor. It is important to ensure that most of the dirt is removed by a doormat before they enter. These mats must be regularly beaten out, cleaned and replaced, so that they remain effective. An old doormat is a liability, having the opposite effect from that intended. It helps if paths for a little distance from the entrance are laid with a few paving slabs to reduce the amount of dust that will be trodden into the church.

Churches that receive a great many visitors either as worshippers or as tourists might consider the usefulness of internal porches. These are commonly found in Europe, particularly in Italy where they are part of the essential furniture. Although not common in Britain they are part of our tradition, and were formerly found both in churches and great houses; in the latter they were for excluding draughts and for the convenience of servants who could deliver materials to rooms without disturbing the occupants. They prevent noise and dust from entering the church directly and could therefore reduce the cleaning requirements.

Clearly these will have an impact on the interior of the church and will have to be carefully considered by the church's architect and the Diocesan Advisory Committee.

If people come in from tarmac roads, they frequently cause stains of tar. These can be removed by applying a 50/50 solution of glycerine and water with a rag and then dabbing the area with a cotton wool swab of eucalyptus oil or a solvent cleaner such as Swarfega. If the oil has penetrated deeply a poultice may be necessary. Chewing gum is best removed by freezing with a block of ice, with care to avoid saturating the surrounding material or freezing your own fingers, after which it can be chipped off with a knife, taking care not to scratch the floor surface below. Holloways produce an aerosol spray which has a similar effect.

As with all cleaning materials, it is wise to err on the side of caution because many cleaning products can be lethal if mixed, and when stored are a notorious fire risk. It is best to tackle stains fresh whenever possible. The biggest problem stains are coffee, wine and oils, which will soak in and be very difficult to get out. In particular powdered detergent and abrasive cleaning methods should never be used without careful thought.

In many ways the principal cause of damage to church floors is the feet of the congregation. As with looking after the fabric of the church building, the maintenance of its floor should be undertaken on the principle of 'little and often'.

FLOOR MATERIALS

Timber boards

In most churches built or restored in the eighteenth and nineteenth centuries, timber boards are often found throughout the church, especially on pew platforms and gallery floors. The finish and size of the boards vary considerably from the small thick blocks of polished parquet laid in diagonals or squares to long parallel boards. If a varnish finish is breaking up there is little alternative to removing the loose flaking material and refinishing the surface with new coats of an oleo-resinous sealer. But commercial sanders must be used with great care. Not only are corners difficult to reach, but sanders remove the surface of the floor timbers and therefore reduce their thickness. One-sixteenth of an inch each time may not seem very much, but if a floor is sanded every ten years, the loss of half an inch may be enough to leave no alternative but the total renewal of the floor after 80 years.

Waxed floors require regular maintenance. If the floor has an established polish, the shine can be renewed with a polisher. Brushes must be clean, and excess wax taken off with white spirit. To remove the surface dust, a woollen cloth should be impregnated with a 50/50 solution of paraffin and vinegar to catch the dust. To retain their efficiency the cloths should be kept in airtight jars, but not in the church: it must be stressed that any use of solvents provide a considerable fire risk. If modern waxes such as Johnson's Traffic Wax are used, they tend to build up and show scuff marks. They must therefore be applied sparingly.

Sealing a floor changes its colour and character, and the total removal of a seal is very difficult. A floor is best kept clean with a dry mop or an electric polisher with a felt pad. Sad areas can be revived slightly by wiping them with a chamois leather impregnated with a solution of white vinegar in warm water (four tablespoons to two gallons) and polished with a soft dry cloth.

Traditionally, wooden floors were rarely polished before the nineteenth century, and many pew platforms are plain timber today. Scrubbing wooden floors is not recommended unless they are really dirty. If it seems essential, then use a bristle brush and do not soak the timber: work in the direction of the grain, using a solution of neutral detergent as a wetting agent; rinse in clean water immediately afterwards and mop dry. Use both buckets simultaneously.

Soaking the timber could easily loosen the boards or blocks. In the unfortunate event of having a floor thoroughly soaked, for example after fire-fighting or a burst pipe, do not touch the swollen wood. With luck the timber will settle back into place as it dries out. If any cleaning is then required, scrubbing with damp soft sand or fuller's earth will give a soft silvery finish. This method will also help to absorb stains. Difficult stains could be tackled individually with fine wire wool and perhaps a little bleach on cotton swabs. A timber floor is very sensitive to the climate in the church. A rapid increase in heat from a new heating system can cause the timber to move, at times with alarming results.

Stone floors

Stone has been used for paving for as long as there have been buildings and is widely used as a traditional flooring material. Everybody imagines that a stone floor lasts almost for ever; unfortunately this is not quite true. As a floor wears it will achieve a significant patina that will add character to the appearance of the church. By comparison, new stone often looks flat or dead, so no old stone should be disregarded just on grounds of appearance.

The choice of stone is governed by the ease with which it can be split or sawn into usable pieces. Stones have been usually selected because of their ease of working. In the mediaeval period transport was a controlling factor which limited the choice. Nowadays that is hardly a factor as stone can be obtained from almost any part of the world. Granite from Portugal is no dearer than granite from Cornwall, although perhaps less appropriate for our traditional church buildings.

Perhaps the best known paving stone is York stone, extracted from carboniferous sandstone south of Leeds and Bradford and around Halifax and Huddersfield. It is quarried in large blocks and can be split or sawn into slabs as thin as 25mm, though between 35mm and 75mm is more usual. The typical delamination that occurs on the top surface need cause no concern, and a weathered texture may even help to increase the non-slip character of the stone. Other sandstones are widely used for paving, and Caithness flags in particular were exported to the south of England in large quantities during the nineteenth century.

Many limestones have been used for flooring but some are too soft to form durable paving. The Purbeck and Portland series are the best known paving stone. Wells Cathedral is paved in part with large slabs of Blue Lias limestone. Some stones such as Wittering pendle, a hard freestone from the oolitic limestone beds north of Stamford, can be set on edge to form pitched paving. This very impermeable stone used to be laid also as a kind of damp-proof course.

Paving slabs can be either riven or sawn. The less even surface of riven slabs develops a patina more quickly but is more difficult to keep clean. The number of so-called marbles found in England are used very effectively for both paving and memorial slabs. They are often used for paving special areas. For example, Ashburton 'marble', which is almost black with thin pink and white veins textured with fossil corals, is used in a side chapel at Guildford Cathedral. Hoptonwood stone is used for the new floor at Birmingham Cathedral. The large black ledger slabs, many of which date from the eighteenth century, are often of marble from Derbyshire, although some may have been imported from Tournai in Belgium.

Granite was seldom used for paving before the nineteenth century, except where specially hard-wearing characteristics were required, as on quays or in industrial buildings, or where it was the only local stone. Modern sawing, however, has made possible its use as a paving material, and a mildly etched surface will increase its non-slip character.

If a new stone floor is to be laid, careful selection of the stone is essential. Traditional paving stones from the United Kingdom are relatively well known, but care must be taken over imported stones. Imported stone laid recently to the new floor of one major church is proving to be too soft for the amount of foot traffic, and it is clear that replacement will be needed quite quickly, even within ten years of laying in heavily used areas.

The most usual problem of existing stone floors is that of loose, cracked or missing stones. Loose stones should be carefully lifted and re-bedded. A cracked but still soundly bedded stone is often best left alone. If relaying is essential, cracked stones can now be repaired with epoxy resins. The period of greatest stress which the repair to the slab will have to withstand is during handling. If a stone is missing a matching one should be found. This can be difficult, and the advice of your architect should be sought. A hole in a pavement is not only dangerous, but places extra strain on the bedding of neighbouring slabs. If a temporary filling of mortar is required, always use a separating medium between the infill and the neighbouring slabs. Paper or polythene can be trimmed flush with the paving and will ensure that the patch can later be removed without disturbing the old floor. Of particular importance is the pointing or joints between the slabs; once this starts to fail the slabs will work loose, begin to rock and eventually crack. Keeping the pointing sound and tight is essential for stone paving to last.

Proprietary domestic cleaners are generally unsuitable for stone floors and should not be used on them. New stone floors can be cleaned either with or without wax, and both methods can give satisfactory results. It is however important to keep any water to an absolute minimum. Dry cleaning will maintain the surface of the stone as it is, but loose and abraded fragments of stone will be lost. If the stones are wax polished the colour and appearance of the floor will change. The polish would be difficult to remove, but it would help to provide a harder wearing surface to the stone. At Guildford Cathedral, where the floor is composed of three stones – Italian marble, Purbeck freestone and a porous French limestone – wax polish is applied to the stone floor with a Johnson 'Traffic' mop and then buffed with a rotary brush pad of a Dixons 35 machine. It should be noted that the cleaners have difficulty with the French limestone.

If a stone floor is allowed to become too wet the salts in or beneath the stone may migrate to the surface. With some stones, such as marble, this will break down and damage the surface finish. If scrubbing is necessary a wet suction machine must be used to dry out the areas as quickly as possible. Washing machines splash, so walls and furniture must be protected. Old stone floors tend to be dusty, especially if they are beginning to break up, but they can be vacuumed using a powerful machine on low power. Be sure to keep carpets and hangings clear of the nozzle.

Some stone slabs are polished and can be treated like wooden floors, but it is not always advisable to start polishing a stone floor because the colour and texture will change. If polishing machines are used, care must be taken not to leave scuff marks on column bases and wall skirtings. Abrasive sanders and grinders should never be used on good quality floors to remove stains and marks. These can generally be lifted by proprietary cleaners such as Bells 1966, or 1967 for marble. A poultice combining an absorbent neutral filler with either pure water or a solvent to form a paste of the consistency of thick double cream will help to shift stubborn marks. The absorbent stone will soak up the moisture from the poultice and as it dries out the poultice will draw it back, carrying the stain with it. Once the poultice has dried out it can be brushed up. A poultice can be made even more effective if the rate of evaporation is slowed down, for example by backing with blotting paper or plastic sheet. The stone must be wetted first or else the stain will simply migrate across it.

Rubber scuff marks can be removed by a 50/50 solution of pure water and white spirit with a spot of washing-up liquid to act as a wetting agent. Dab the mixture on and rinse it off locally with clean water.

Metal

Metal is used as part of the construction on church floors as ducts, vents or inspection plates. In many nineteenth-century church floors, the patterned grilles of the heating ducts form a surprisingly large part of the total area. The grilles must be secure and safe, and broken ones can often be mended so that the overall appearance is kept uniform. If they are clogged with paint they can be removed and cleaned to bring out the decorative detail using a non-alkaline paint stripper following any health and safety guidelines laid down by the manufacturers.

The other type of metalwork found on church floors is monumental brasses and these are treated in a totally different way. Every effort should be made to prevent people walking on them, but if this is not possible then a suitable covering should be laid over the top, such as a good quality underfelt and carpet. A layer of plastic or similar synthetic material should not be used, as microclimates can be set up causing the metal to corrode. Coarse material, for example, coconut matting, must not be used as dirt can be trapped in the fibres and then act as an abrasive on the surface of the brass.

Over the years brasses may become loosened in their settings, or discoloured with corrosion. Cleaning, restoration and resetting must only be undertaken by skilled, experienced conservators. Light surface cleaning and applications of protective coatings may be carried out by non-professionals but only under the guidance of experienced conservators.

Clay brick and tile

Fired clay products have been used for flooring for centuries, and we have already summarised their history. In churches they fall into the following categories: low-fired plain clay tiles and bricks; decorative low-fired clay tiles; pressed tiles; plain glazed tiles; and patterned glazed tiles. The problems of repair and conservation are very similar with all these materials. The choice of method will depend on the importance of the floor, on which advice should be sought from the Diocesan Advisory Committee.

The encaustic and patterned tiles provided by the mediaeval industries are an important and largely recognised part of our ecclesiastical heritage. The rate at which they seem to be wearing gives cause for great concern. Floors suffer from wear in several different ways: furniture dragged frequently over the surface will remove the patterned slip; rising damp will cause the migration of soluble salts, and their crystallisation on the surface will cause damage. Damp will also cause the white clay inlay to bubble forward and become soft and powdery, which poses very difficult problems of conservation. A recent addition to the list is the application of a modern sealant to give the tiles a permanent wet look which shows up the pattern. This material will inevitably cause irreparable damage and should not be used. The bedding and fixing of these tiles must not be done with a

Portland cement-based mix, but with a traditional lime-based bedding. If chips need to be made up, a coloured lime putty is the best material to use. Broken tiles may be repaired with an adhesive that is reversible. If soluble salts are present they may be professionally removed with de-ionised water. If in any doubt, ask at your local museum or the relevant branch of the Area Museum Service, who may be willing to provide free or subsidised help.

Worn plain clay tile and brick floors develop a fine patina which ought not to be disturbed without good reason. They are also very difficult to lift and relay. The tiles are often so soft that only the integrity of the floor keeps it all together. Since repairs are difficult to achieve, it is best, if a floor must be relaid, to try to group the historical material together and relay the rest with as close a match as possible. Modern French and Spanish unglazed clay tiles are often similar in texture and colour, but they may not correspond in size. A number of craft potters in England are also now making reproduction tiles either on a regular basis or to special order.

Pressed clay tiles of the nineteenth and twentieth centuries are much more dense and hard-wearing, but they often work loose from their bedding. The movement or loss of one tile puts a strain on the neighbouring tiles. It is important that the integrity of a pavement is maintained. If the tile is only loose and the bedding is still sound it can be reset in a mix of sand, lime and casein. Finely sieved lime putty combined with skimmed milk and mixed to a double cream consistency will sometimes be adequate but should only be used in small areas because of the risk of bacteria attack.

In very rare cases it is sometimes necessary to salvage areas of tiles for re-use. With lime-bedded tiles that is seldom a problem, but for floors set in hard cement it is often very difficult to separate the bedding on the back of the tiles from the underlying material. It is not practical to attempt to separate the tile from its background except under laboratory conditions with diamond-tipped saws. Rescues must therefore be very carefully planned, and should incorporate a full survey and record. Either a specialist contractor should be used, or a very precise specification should be prepared by the architect. There has in recent years been a revival in the making of pressed tiles following Victorian examples, and it is now possible to obtain replacements for missing tiles.

It was frequently the practice to apply wax polish on tiles, and if it is essential a 50/50 solution of linseed oil and paraffin wax will produce an acceptable finish. However, it is often best not to wax polish as it will usually build up very quickly to a substantial thickness. Although it is quite possible to remove the wax, care must be taken because it is likely that the solvents may well attack the clay of the tiles. Always test a small area first, and continue to work in small areas thereafter. The glazes in particular can be very vulnerable. Advice can be sought from the Area Museum Service or the Diocesan Advisory Committee. Attempts have recently been made to remove the accretion of wax and linseed oil on a mediaeval tile floor with methyl alcohol and methylene chloride applied with cotton wool and cleaned off with white spirit on swabs and dried with a warm air blower. The tiles were then finished with a white micro-crystalline wax. Some experts have commented that a change seems to have occurred on that pavement. Any conservation action may change the colour of tiles. For robust Victorian floors the possibility of steam cleaning could be investigated.

Jointless floors

Floors with a uniform surface are generally made of a hard-wearing material carried in a spreading agent which is laid on a firm base such as concrete slab or concrete screed. If correctly laid such floors nearly all have the advantage of being hard-wearing and simple to maintain. Some, such as terrazzo and granolithic paving, are inherently inflexible and tend to crack as a result of poor preparation, movement of the slab or failure of the bond. Repair and patching of these floors can present a problem, and professional guidance should be obtained. Never clean asphalt or bituminous floors with hot water or soap, which will make the floor slippery. Wax polish or sealer also must not be used because they will soften the material of the floor.

Sheet floors

All sheet floors must be laid on a smooth base, otherwise they will lose their even surface. Apart from carpets, the commonest sheet flooring materials are linoleum, vinyl and plastic sheet, rubber, cork and composition blocks.

Linoleum

Linoleum, invented in 1863 by Frederick Walton, is made from a compound of natural ingredients baked at low temperature on to a supporting material, usually jute or hessian. Modern linoleum is a strong hard-wearing floor covering with a good range of colours and marbled effects.

Flooring grade cork

Cork is a good flooring material because the thicker grades wear well and it is warm, resilient and quiet. It should be properly laid and sealed, but it is not appropriate if underfloor heating is used.

Vinyl

Vinyl is available in sheets or tiles in a wide variety of patterns, colours and textures. The thicker cushioned vinyls are quiet, resilient and warm underfoot but the thinner ones can be cold and hard. They are resistant to water, oil, fat and most domestic chemicals but they are very vulnerable to burns and abrasion by grit. Vinyl will become brittle if the building is underheated.

Rubber and synthetic rubber

Rubber floor coverings are common in places of public assembly. They are hard-wearing and are available in a range of colours and textures. The edges of rubber floors need especially careful attention.

Composition floors

Composition blocks are a useful alternative to timber in some circumstances. The composition is formed by compressing a mixture of softwood particles, mineral fillers and pigment with water to form individual blocks which have a keyed surface on the underside. A sound and solid base, usually concrete slabs, is essential. The blocks are set in a 3:1 sand/cement slurry and well bedded in, the joints are grouted and the top surface sanded clean and sealed with a sealer, usually a polyurethane compound. Although maintenance is straight-forward, the colour and texture of these floors is not suitable for all buildings.

The original selection of floor covering material is likely to have been the choice of the designer, but it is important to find out what sort of floor a church has. The proper cleaning material for linoleum, for example, is very different from that for sheet vinyl.

Asphalt, bituminous vinyl sheet and thermoplastic sheet are all cleaned in the same way. Regular maintenance is to sweep, preferably using damp sawdust, to mop with warm water and a mild detergent (one oz to two gallons) and then buff to restore the sheen. A water-based plastic emulsion polish should be applied in heavily used areas before the existing polish wears away, taking care to avoid a build-up in lightly used areas. If necessary a thick layer of polish can be stripped and the treatment repeated. Soap will make the floor slippery, and should not be used; nor should hot water over 180°F, nor liquid wax polish: both would soften the floor.

Linoleum, rubber sheet and tiles have a slightly different cleaning routine. A water/plastic emulsion finish is now commonly used. It is very important never to use large quantities of water or strong alkali detergents for regular maintenance. Wax polish is also unsuitable.

Carpets

Carpets are becoming increasingly common in parish churches. But there are two opposed schools of thought on the subject. To some they provide a friendly warm atmosphere, contributing colour and softening the acoustics. To others they attempt to make the church more like a hotel foyer or a domestic interior and strike a discordant note. It will also be argued that they will wear badly and soon look shabby, and that they will dampen the acoustics so that more money must be spent on electrical gadgets to fortify the sound. There are extreme cases which justify both views. As with all aspects of buildings, selection is a matter of compromise, and a suitable choice for a modern church may prove to be an expensive disaster for an older one.

In a typical mediaeval church with flagstones and no damp-proof course it is traditional and practical to use a coconut, rush or sisal matting, with good quality carpet at the altar steps. The coarse open texture of these mats allow the floor to breathe. They will all deteriorate if they are allowed to become too dry, so occasional damping with a fine low-mist spray is worthwhile. Every year they should be lifted so that the dirt beneath can be swept up. The choice of type of carpet is broad and confusing, but basically lies between traditional and modern types. The durability of a carpet does not depend upon its brand name but on its inherent qualities – its density, its resilience and the weight of its pile. The quicker the pile recovers from an impression, the denser and more resilient the carpet. Short, dense fibre carpets are the most durable. Long strands and big loops look bulky but weigh less and are not so durable. Carpets will have a varying percentage of wool to synthetic material, depending upon the wearing characteristic. Modern synthetic fibres are improving all the time.

The difference between an Axminster and a Wilton is not unlike the difference between plain and purl in knitting. The distinction lies in the stitch, not in the quality. Axminster and Wilton both resemble plaited or woven fabric, but at the same time are knotted into a pile. Tufted carpet on the other hand is made from canvas fed into an enormous sewing machine with thousands of needles making loops which are then cut into pile, thick or thin according to the adjustment of the machine.

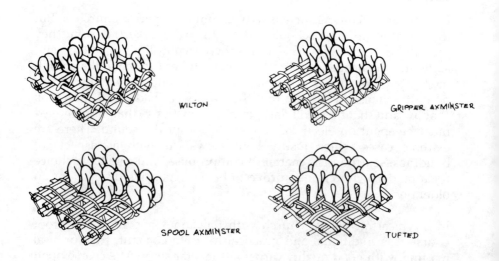

WILTON

GRIPPER AXMINSTER

SPOOL AXMINSTER

TUFTED

Carpet types

26

The use of modern computers now makes specially designed carpets quite realistic and not unduly expensive. If the area is over 200 square metres there is often no extra charge.

Non-wool fibres are now used frequently in carpets:

Acrylic is the most wool-like in appearance. It wears well but because it is not as resilient as wool, dirt shows more readily and it is not as easy to clean.

Modacrylic is more expensive than acrylic and has better flame-resistant qualities. But the fibre is difficult to dye and the range of colours is therefore more limited.

Nylon and Polyamide have a high-wear resistance, but some manufacturers use only a low pile weight, giving a carpet that looks well for a shorter time. To be satisfactory they ought to weigh at least 560 grams per square metre (20oz per square yard). Some are specially treated with an anti-soil process to repel dirt. They are fine until the treatment starts to age, and then they are worse than untreated carpets. The treatment can, however, be re-applied. Problems of static electricity can be overcome by incorporating metal or carbon fibres into the weaves and keeping the humidity of the carpet under control.

Polyester is used for long-pile carpets, called shag. It has a lower resistance than acrylic.

Polypropylene is hard-wearing and cheap and is often blended with other materials. It does not readily show dirt but has a high flammability and is not self-extinguishing. It is often used in backings because it absorbs little moisture.

Viscose-Rayon is cheap and not very hard-wearing. It is often mixed with other materials to add bulk. It has low resilience and low dirt resistance. Some types are easily flammable.

Haircords are slightly cheaper and provide a good covering for larger areas. Synthetic cords can, however, become shiny with use.

Handmade carpets are good for special areas, but because of their smaller size they tend to fit into the more ambitious embroidery projects.

Choosing a colour and pattern is a subjective matter which can arouse great conflict of opinion. It is essential to look at good-sized samples in the church. Plain carpets should be avoided because they will show stains and shading. The direction of the pile is also important: in some areas it can be reversed to give a different tone to the carpet colours. Newly laid carpets tend to produce fluff for the first few weeks, and should be gently brushed. Thereafter they should be regularly vacuumed at least once a week to prevent dirt becoming embedded at the base of the pile where it can rub and cut loose the fibres, resulting in bare patches. Fully fitted carpets are not recommended because in many churches they will be difficult in awkward corners. They may also not be appropriate, either because of the effect on the appearance of the building or because the floor may contain tiles or memorials which ought to remain visible. Some parishes suggest that panels (or windows) of carpet can be made, to be lifted if anyone wishes to view the memorials, but this is really neither practical nor desirable.

The advantages which are often claimed for carpets need to be carefully examined. Carpets will provide both psychological warmth and thermal insulation; but they cannot create actual warmth, and if insulation is essential it can be provided better and more economically in other ways. Lightweight carpets have minimal sound-absorbent qualities; but heavy-duty carpets can significantly alter the acoustic character of a church.

Carpets for places of assembly are designed in terms of performance for hygiene and convenience; but a church is a place set apart for the higher purpose of worship both communal and individual. Some PCCs may decide to try and create a feeling of comfort as an important aspect of their parish's style of worship. At first sight carpet is cheaper than almost all other permanent flooring materials but is this difference really substantial in the long term? The aesthetic impact must also be carefully considered.

Carpets should be laid on even floors. Often to give a good base the floor will need to be levelled, or a special levelling screed must be laid. If the carpet is to last any significant period it must be of good quality. Guarantees, for what they are worth, often mention 3,000 days. In a public building this would mean about twelve years. Many hotels budget for eight-yearly replacement. Churches have a different sort of use, usually in short intense bursts, so it would not be unreasonable to double the possible lifespan. But that still means replacement once in every generation.

Many solid floors are over a century old – some considerably more. It can be argued that carpet represents a short-term economic advantage that will pass the burden of replacement to future generations. Carpet must be laid properly, especially if it is fitted, and once laid it must be looked after. If laid on even floor, normal vacuuming once a week will be sufficient, with a shampoo occasionally. Carpet cleaners should comply with BS4088, but *always* test a sample area first. Do not use soap powder or ammonia as the alkali may cause the colours to run. It is important to leave the pile facing the correct direction and to keep people off the carpet until it is dry.

Preferable to a shampoo is to use water extraction cleaners. These lay a non-foaming detergent solution under pressure and then suck up 90 per cent of the solution immediately. It is best to choose a warm and good drying day and well ventilate the church to encourage drying. It is important to protect all metal feet of furniture and be careful not to over-wet the carpet.

A surprising number of churches have carpets of historic interest. These are often good European or Oriental rugs. If in doubt, expert advice about their quality and value should always be taken. Any spillage or stain on the carpet should be dealt with as soon as possible. How the rugs lie on the floor is also important. A good quality rug should have its own underlay. Light rugs can be secured to a hard floor with a rubber mesh backing or nylon bonding strip which will both avoid dangerous slipping and stop the rugs 'walking'. But be sure there is nothing of value on the floor beneath the rug. Small rugs are also vulnerable to theft, so it is important the parish inventories should include photographs of such items, which they seldom do.

All carpeting is expensive and difficult to patch. One of the keys to the long life of either rugs or fitted carpets is the underlay. Carpet paper will help to prevent damp rising up into the carpet or underlay and will prevent dust rising between floorboards or from concrete slabs. Underlay will also prolong the life of any carpet, and on uneven surfaces will help to spread and cushion the humps and bumps which cause uneven wear. Underlays should come right to the edge of the rug or carpet and not be trimmed back. Animal fibre underlay has a high resilience and should have a weight of about 1kg per square metre (2.5lb per square yard). Always avoid the use of cheap foam rubber or composition-backed underlays and carpets. They deterioriate unevenly, cause solid floors to sweat, and can stick to the floor surface, making removal a terrible task.

In order to even out the wear, rugs and loose carpets should be turned on a regular basis. It is worthwhile, and the life of many stair carpets has been prolonged by this, to move the carpet a few inches every so often. Where church furniture sits on a carpet it should be protected with simple coloured strips of timber. Heavy chests, pianos and chairs can do considerable damage. If the carpet is of high quality, consideration can be given to a drugget or covering to protect it from light, dust and wear which could then be removed for services. Never use plastic coverings because they can cause permanent damage to carpets, and may even encourage mildew. Covers should be thoroughly cleaned every year to avoid damage by trapped grit and dirt.

* * * * * * *

Whether church floors are of antiquarian interest or of modern convenience, the best answer to their care would be to keep people from walking on them; there is no doubt that the greatest damage is caused by people's feet! But since we must walk on our church floors, some way must be found for caring for them to preserve them for the future.

FLOORS AND THE DISABLED

It is not the role of this booklet to cover the relationship between the church, its fitments and the disabled. Disabled people have varying demands and varying expections of church buildings.

However, the critical priorities with disabled people are:

1. Avoid unexpected hazards.

2. Provide good illumination of steps and avoid pattern in carpets that camouflage steps.

3. Ensure that handrails are correctly provided and securely fixed, capable of taking a person's weight.

4.   If ramps are provided, ensure that they are accessible to wheelchairs and support frames. Allow for adequate turning circles at the top and bottom.

5.   Generally home-made facilities are not a good idea. Consult an architect and the DAC before commissioning any alterations.

SOURCES FOR MATERIALS MENTIONED IN THE TEXT

G.E. Holloway and Son, 12 Carlisle Road, Colindale, London, NW9

A. Bell and Company, Thornton Road, Kingsthorpe, Northampton, NN2 6LT

Jeyes, PO Box 20, Cressex, High Wycombe, Buckinghamshire, NP12 3TL

Johnson Wax Limited, Frimley Green, Camberley, Surrey, GU6 5AJ

A chemist will supply glycerine, eucalyptus oil, borax, fuller's earth, speolite and hydrogen peroxide.

Do-it-yourself shops will supply mineral spirits, talc, Swarfega, Polyclens Plus, Nitromors, water soluble paint remover, Relston wood bleach.